THE BEAUTY OF
FLOWERS

THE BEAUTY OF
FLOWERS

MARY LAWRENCE,
JANE NEWDICK &
JUDY TAYLOR

EAST
COAST
MARKETING

The
Book People!

CREDITS

MANAGING EDITOR: *Jilly Glassborow*

EDITED BY: *Veronica Ross*

PHOTOGRAPHY BY: *Jane Newdick, Richard Paines
and Helen Pask*

DESIGN AND ARTWORK BY: *Pauline Bayne*

TYPESET BY: *SX Composing Ltd.*

COLOUR SEPARATION BY: *P&W Graphics, Pte. Ltd.*

PRINTED IN SLOVENIA

CONTENTS

Part 1

Fresh Flower Arranging

*F*lowers have been used for decorative purposes since time immemorial. Today, the craft has undergone something of a revival and now most people probably have a plant or a vase of flowers in their home. There is no great mystique attached to arranging flowers. A simple posy can look as stunning as a more lavish arrangement, and once you have mastered the basic techniques you can go on to design your own displays.

When selecting flowers, choose blooms with crisp foliage, strong stems and firm flower buds. Re-cut the stems when you get home, and give the flowers a long drink before transferring them to shallow water and a warm room. To preserve the life of your blooms, add a spoonful of sugar, an aspirin tablet or even lemonade to the water, or purchase preservatives from a florist.

You will need some pieces of basic equipment before you start. A pair of florists' scissors is a good investment and a sharp knife is helpful for cutting away foliage. Florists' foam will keep your display in position. It readily absorbs water and just needs to be soaked before using. For heavier stems crumple wire mesh inside the container. A pinholder may also be useful when designing an arrangement using a limited number of flowers.

Flowers can transform the appearance of a room, so think carefully about your display. Consider harmony and balance, colour and shape before you begin. Choose blooms to complement your decor or to enhance the container. Use contrasting colours to add depth or toning colours for a coordinated display.

Flowers never fail to delight, and the displays featured in this chapter will inspire you to create your own colourful, fragrant designs.

$\mathcal{D}$UET FOR PEONIES

20 pink peonies
3 bunches of blue cornflowers
6 sprays of eucalyptus
String & two jugs

he floral design on these pretty blue and pink patterned jugs is beautifully complemented by the choice of peonies and rich blue cornflowers for this elegant tied (hostess) bunch. Arrange a fan shape of eucalyptus foliage in the hand and secure with string. Bind the peonies firmly into the bunch following the shape of the foliage and adding in extra budding peonies, foliage and open peonies as you work. Add a flourish of cornflowers down one side and finish with a short bunch at the base of the display. Tie off the string and insert the arrangement into a jug. For the smaller jug display, cut down four peony stems so that the heads fall over the rim of the jug. To finish off, position the three bunches of cornflowers in the centre of the display.

$\mathcal{O}$*VERTURE*

~

15 yellow ranuculus
1 bunch of yellow genista
5 orange tulips
3 blue irises
Ivy trails
Patterned jug

$\mathcal{T}$his bright and pretty cottage style display will be a welcome addition to any kitchen. The vivid colours on the floral patterned jug have been carefully picked out in the use of the fresh flowers. The narrow neck of the jug firmly grips the display and helps to secure the flowers in position.

Begin by arranging a posy of ranuculus in the hand. Clean and trim the stems and place them in the jug of water. Add an outline of genista and position the irises to give depth to the design. Insert the orange tulips at random throughout the arrangement to give an extra burst of colour. Finally tuck in wispy trails of ivy to spill over the rim of the jug and to add a final decorative touch to the design.

$\int$PRING CHORUS

~

2 bunches of daffodils
Daffodil leaves
3 bunches of forget-me-nots
Woven basket
Wire mesh
Plastic container to fit basket

A wicker basket provides a perfect country setting for this charming display of spring daffodils and early forget-me-nots. Before starting your display, line the wicker basket with a plastic container to protect it and fill with crunched wire mesh.

Position one bunch of daffodils at the back of the container adding in the daffodil foliage to give a natural look. Group the forget-me-nots into several small bunches and insert throughout the basket with some tucked into the front so that they just peep over the edge. Cut down the stems of the remaining bunch of daffodils, and position them at random in among the forget-me-nots to complete this picturesque country setting.

$\mathcal{I}$RIS REPRISE

～

3 yellow irises
5 blue irises
Bunch of mixed narcissi
Bunch of primroses
Periwinkle flowers
Hazel catkins
Ivy foliage
Floral teapot
Wire mesh

$\mathcal{T}$he pretty floral pattern on this teapot has been cleverly picked out in the use of the blue and yellow iris. The bold outlines and strong colours of the iris complement the rich honeyed tones of the pine dresser.

Fill the teapot with crunched wire mesh. Position the iris so that they lean in the direction of the teapot spout, with the shortest stems in the centre of the pot to form the focal point. Intermingle the arrangement with the catkins and place the narcissi at random through the display. To finish, tuck in the periwinkle flowers, primroses and the ivy leaves.

ℰNSEMBLE

∽

5 bells of Ireland (Moluccella)
5 white sweet peas
5 white freesias
3 white stocks
1 white carnation
2 sprays of green love-lies-bleeding
Collection of blue bottles

These pretty, old fashioned medicine bottles enhance the pure line of this cool summer display of green and white flowers. This arrangement looks especially attractive silhouetted against a pale background.

Insert the bells of Ireland into the tallest bottles at the back of the arrangement to give the display height and a sweeping background shape. Place the feathery sweet peas in the smaller bottles at the front, along with the freesias and stocks. The solid white carnation adds depth to the design. Position the soft sprays of love-lies-bleeding at the very front to gently sweep down to meet the crisp white tablecloth.

PEACH QUINTET

~

15 peach floribunda roses
7 sprays of peach carnations
7 sprays of pale peach carnations
Variegated ivy leaves
Posy bowl
Florists' foam

This charming, fresh looking posy of peach coloured roses combined with carnations looks very pleasing. The muted shades of the peach blooms match the decor of this room perfectly.

Fill the posy bowl with soaked florists' foam. Place ivy leaves around the edge so that they overlap a little. Cut a single rose bud stem to one and a third the height of the container and position in the centre of the bowl. Gradually add in the remaining roses while turning the bowl round to create an even effect. Use the open and budding carnations to fill in, placing the two shades of peach blooms at random throughout the arrangement, but taking care not to overlap the base leaves.

$\mathcal{P}$RELUDE

~

20 cerise hyacinths
20 white daffodils
20 muscari
Serving dish
Wire mesh
Florist' foam
Water resistant tape

$\mathcal{T}$his elegant serving dish is a perfect container for a pyramid flower design and makes a superb decoration for a buffet table. Begin by forming the florists' foam into a cone shape and then wrap in wire mesh. Attach to the dish with water resistant tape, and soak well in water.

Position a hyacinth bud at the top of the cone and, slowly turning the dish towards you, add in the remaining hyacinths graduating in size down towards the edge of the dish to create a pyramid shape. Tuck in the white daffodils between the sprays of hyacinths and finally add the blue muscari to define the shape and provide colour contrast.

$\mathcal{C}$OUNTRY REEL

~

9 pink ranunculus
11 love-in-a-mist
3 sprays of pinks (Dianthus x allwoodii)
Ivy foliage
Maple foliage
String
Jug

$\mathcal{W}$ith a little time and care a simple bunch of garden flowers can be transformed into a charming hostess bunch fit to adorn any sitting room. These pink blooms mixed with green foliage look particularly pretty.

Separate the flowers and foliage into mixed groups. Cut each group to a different length and strip the lower leaves from the stems. Start by tying string to the tallest bunch of flowers and then tie in the smaller bunches, turning the bunch as you work. Place the most dominant colour at the base of the design. Make sure there is a balanced all round effect and break up any solid areas of colour or foliage by tying in single stems of foliage.

ℬUTTERFLY

∾

Several small branches of apple blossom
5 pink tulips
Chinese bowl
Large metal pinholder
Florists' foam

The natural simplicity and freshness of flowering apple blossom combined with pale pink tulips adds a timeless tranquility to this oriental setting. The Chinese bowl gives the display an authentic look.

Use a large metal pinholder in the bottom of the bowl to act as a balance and fill with well soaked florists' foam. Strip the bark from the lower stems of the apple branches and crush the stems with a hammer to aid drinking. Position two branches at the back of the bowl at an oblique angle. Place the shorter branches at the front of the bowl at the same angle. Add the final branch of blossom and position it so that it bends down to touch the table. Starting from the left, and following the line of the final branch, position the tulips to make a central focal point.

$\mathcal{T}$EA FOR TWO

∽

20 white ranunculus
Sprays of hedge parsley
Ivy foliage
Green plastic covered florists' mesh
Green glass dish
Florists' tape

$\mathcal{I}$n the early stages of flowering, white ranunculus have a greenish tinge which combines beautifully with the sprays of hedge parsley and ivy to make this charming display a welcome addition to your afternoon tea table.

Secure the crushed mesh into the glass dish with florists' tape. Cut one ranunculus stem to two and a half times the height of the sundae dish and position in the centre of the display. Surround the central stem with the remaining ranunculus which cascade down and over the edge of the dish. Add ivy leaves among the blooms to give crispness and depth to the design, and fill in with the sprays of hedge parsley and the remaining ranunculus buds.

CONCERTO

11 pink antirrhinums
13 pink carnations
5 pink zinnias
7 sprays of peach carnations
2 bunches of deep pink sweet peas
5 scabious (pincushion flower)
7 agapanthus
Sprays of sprengeri fern
Crystal vase
Wire mesh
Florists' tape

This stunning display of predominately pink flowers looks surprisingly pretty against a vivid pink floral background. To start bend a circle of wire mesh over the top of the vase and secure in position with tape. Build up a fan-shaped outline with the antirrhinum, sweet peas and spray carnation. Position the large pink carnations to create a focal point and arrange sweet peas and fern to spill over the front of the vase. Use zinnias, scabious and agapanthus to give depth and added colour to the display.

$\mathcal{C}$ARMEN

∾

6 stems of red gladioli
7 stems of bells of Ireland (Moluccella)
Marguerites
Rectangular glass container
Medium sized piece of charcoal

$\mathcal{T}$he simple rectangular glass container used here complements the dramatic quality of the gladioli and continues the line of the design under water adding a pleasing contrast to the blaze of colour.

Fill the container three-quarters full with water. Clean all the flower stems as they will be visible under water. Cut one gladioli stem to three times the height of the container and position so that it leans to the left at the back. Trim five gladioli so that they graduate downwards in size and position them along the back of the vase with bells of Ireland placed in between. Cut short the remaining gladioli and place at the front right edge. Use the marguerites to fill the front of the display. Wedge the charcoal at the back of the vase to keep the water clear.

$\mathcal{H}$ARMONY

~

12 stems of mauve freesias
12 mauve roses
10 mauve sweet peas
20 purple anemones
Ivy foliage
Eucalyptus foliage
Silver dish
Glass bowl
Florists' foam and florists' tape

$\mathcal{T}$he beautiful floral fretwork on this silver dish looks stunning against the dark wood of the dining table and harmonizes well with the mauve and purple blooms used for this informal table arrangement.

Place a glass bowl filled with foam inside the silver dish and secure with florists' tape. Place the foliage around the edge of the dish allowing the ivy to trail onto the table. Insert a rose in the centre of the bowl and position the remaining roses to graduate down to the edge. Add the sweet peas, freesias and dark anemones among the roses.

ORCHESTRATION

~

12 stems of delphinium
18 yellow antirrhinum
5 heads of blue/mauve hydrangeas
Large vase
Wire mesh
Florists' securing tape

C hoose a tall sturdy vase and bold elegant flowers to create this stunning floor standing arrangement, which will complement any sitting room or hallway. Loosely pack the vase with crumpled wire mesh. Bend a circle of wire mesh to overlap the rim of the vase and secure in position with florists' tape. Fill with water.

Place the tallest delphinium stem in the centre of the vase. Position the other delphiniums in front and to the side of the central stem, graduating downwards in height to create an even effect. Intersperse the delphiniums with yellow antirrhinum following the line of the design, and to complete the arrangement place the hydrangea blooms around the neck of the vase.

$\mathcal{S}$YMPHONY

❧

7 stems of delphinium
7 pink peonies & 9 pale pink roses
6 white antirrhinum
4 stems of bells of Ireland (Moluccella)
3 stems of green love-lies-bleeding
3 sprays of pink alstroemeria
5 stems of astrantia
Oval Victorian tureen
Wire mesh & string

$\mathcal{T}$his stunning display captures all the beauty and freshness of a summer garden. Crunch a piece of wire mesh into the tureen and secure with string. Build up height in the centre of the display with a single tall delphinium stem. Place the remaining delphiniums, the bells of Ireland and antirrhinum around the central stem so that they curve gracefully towards the table. Place three peonies in the centre to give depth to the design and fill in with the single blooms of roses and peonies. Position alstroemeria and astrantia to soften the outline.

ORCHID SONATA

6 sprays of striped & red arachnis orchids
2 sprays of white orchids
1 spray of red & white dendrobium
Red leaved foliage Smoke tree (Cotinus coggygria)
Small brass watering can
Florists' foam

These readily available and lasting orchids have a fascinating and distinctive beauty of their own and this simple arrangement emphasizes the detail of each individual bloom.

Pack soaked florists' foam into a decorative miniature brass watering can. Place the red and striped arachnis orchids at the back of the container following the slope of the spout. Trim the buds from some of the white orchids and place them to the front right of the arrangement to follow the line through to the top of the spout. Place the dendrobium orchids in the centre of the arrangement and fill in with small sprays of red foliage.

ℛHAPSODY

11 red antirrhinums
7 red peonies
5 sweet Williams
6 white stocks
1 bunch of red sweet peas
White poplar foliage
Large decorative jug & wire mesh

The striking display of vivid red and pure white flowers beautifully complements the attractive floral pattern on the vase. Begin by crunching the wire mesh securely into the jug. Cut down one antirrhinum stem to twice the height of the jug and position it at the centre back of the jug.

Arrange the remaining antirrhinum around the curve of the jug and intermingle the poplar foliage. Place a swathe of peonies from back to centre and repeat using sweet peas. The white stocks introduce pleasing colour contrast throughout the centre of the design. Fill in with sweet William and poplar foliage to spill over the rim of the jug.

CHRISTMAS CAROL

~

22 red carnations & 20 red spray carnations
7 bells of Ireland (Moluccella) & 7 green love-lies-bleeding
10 red alstroemeria & 7 auratum lilies
10 sprays of red arachnis orchids
Branches of tortured willow
Gold ribbon 4ins (10cms) wide & gold spray paint
Large heavy oval container
2 small heavy oval containers
Ivy, ruscus & pine foliage
Florists' foam & waterproof tape

Fill the containers with soaked florists' foam and secure with tape. Spray the lilies and willow branches with gold paint. Form the ruscus into a fan shaped outline in the central container. Build up the shape with mixed red flowers using the gold lilies as a central line. Place a gold bow at the centre base of the container so it trails over the mantelpiece. Add in the sprays of ruscus. Position the willow in the side containers and intersperse with sprays of orchids. Cover the base with pine foliage. Finish off by adding in remaining gold lilies.

Part 2

Dried Flower Designs

*I*n recent years the popularity of dried flowers has soared, and now all manner of stunning dried blooms are available. The finished displays are packed with colour, and can last for years. Mixed bunches of flowers can now be purchased in department stores, florists, and specialist shops, although the cheapest way of pursuing this hobby is to dry your own blooms.

There are several ways of drying flowers but air drying is probably the easiest. Bind the flowers into bunches and leave them hanging upside down in a warm, dark place for one to four weeks, depending on the type of plant. Specialist drying agents are also available. One of the easiest to use is silica gel which comes in the form of white crystals. Place a layer of crystals into the base of an airtight box and place the wired flowerheads on top. Using a spoon, carefully cover the flowers with crystals. Close the container and leave for a couple of days.

You will need to purchase some basic equipment before starting, such as dry foam to support your arrangement and various types of wire. Stub wires are straight lengths of wire used for supporting single flowerheads or binding plants together into small bunches. Reel wire is used for wreaths where a continuous length of wire is needed, and finer silver wire is used for delicate work, for example binding posies. You may also need wire mesh and pin-holders for support, florists' adhesive to secure the supports, and clear glue to stick individual flowers in place.

When planning your arrangement, choose flowers to harmonize with your room or to enhance the design of a favourite vase. Start by copying some of the designs in this chapter until you feel confident enough to try out your own ideas and create your own original arrangements.

$\int$ILVER POSY

∾

12 stems of lily of the valley
15 stems of muscari & 9 cornflowers
5 pansies & 3 astrantia
7 narcissi & 2 stems of pulmonaria
3 stems of spurge
Salad burnett leaves (burnet)
Florists' stub wire
Silica gel & plastic box with lid
Silver bowl

This pretty miniature display has been carefully preserved in silica gel. Cut down the flower stems and push a stub wire into each stem. Pour an inch of silica gel crystals into a plastic box. Put the flowers in the box and gently sieve more crystals over them until the flowers are covered under a layer at least ½in (1cm) thick. Seal and leave for 2 or 3 days. Lift the flowers out carefully, and remove the crystals with a paint brush. Fill the bowl with crushed wire mesh, and gently insert the wired flowers to build up a posy shape. Use dried foliage to cover any visible wires.

$\mathcal{B}$LUE SKIES

∽

11 stems of delphinium
7 pink peonies
5 stems of Eucalyptus cinerea (silver dollar tree)
4 stems of Eucalyptus globulus (Tasmanian blue gum)
Wire mesh
Florists' adhesive tape
Glass vase

The design of this pale blue glass vase inspires and dictates the shape of this charming arrangement. The flowers follow the line of the vase, falling into a graceful shape. Cut a piece of wire mesh to fit over the top of the vase and secure in place with adhesive tape. Carefully position the delphiniums to follow their natural shape and fill in with the soft sprays of eucalyptus. Next, position the peonies to give depth to the design. Finally, arrange short stems of eucalyptus to spread over the front of the vase.

WALL FLOWERS

∾

6 peonies & 3 peonies in bud
1 bunch of white larkspur
1 bunch of pink larkspur
1 bunch of deep pink helichrysum (strawflower or everlasting)
1 bunch of pink broom blooms
1 bunch of willow & myrtle
Shallow basket
Florists' dry foam & adhesive tape
Fast drying clear glue & stub wire
2 plastic pinholders & fixative

This wall display looks stunning arranged in a shallow basket. Thread wire through the top of the basket to make a hanger. Using green fixative, secure the plastic pinholders to one side of the base of the basket. Place foam onto the pinholder and secure with adhesive tape. Following the line of the basket, insert larkspur stems into the foam. Wire the other flowers into short bunches and fill in. Position peonies to form a central focal line and place the helichrysum below the peonies to create harmony and depth.

VICTORIAN POSY

∾

7 pink roses
5 pink helichrysum (strawflower or everlasting)
10 small poppy seed heads
1 bunch of peach & 1 bunch of bleached glixias
1 bunch of bleached broom blooms
1 bunch of glycerined male fern
Florists' silver reel wire
Florists' stub wire & stem tape
Cream lace & peach ribbon

Dried flowers in various shades of pink and peach combine beautifully to make this wedding posy. Divide the broom blooms into short bunches and wire a stub wire to each bunch. Repeat with the glixias, and with each single flower and seed head. Cover the wires with tape. Start the posy by binding silver wire to a wired rose. Surround the rose with a circle of bleached glixias and bind in. Add a circle of roses, helichrysum and poppy heads, and a circle of broom bloom. Twist the stub wires together to make a handle. Bind in a circle of peach and bleached glixias and fern. Decorate with ribbon and lace.

$\mathcal{S}$UMMER GLORY

12 burgundy-edged carnations
12 pink Japanese anemones
5 sprays of spiraea
3 purple pom-pom dahlia
1 bunch of purple & 1 bunch of white statice
Dried moss
Florists' adhesive tape
Florists' reel wire, tape & stub wire
Cling film (plastic wrap)
Posy bowl

This charming design has all the appeal of a fresh flower arrangement. To preserve your display and to retain the natural colours of the flowers, dry the individual blooms in silica gel before you start on your design (see page 46). Line the bowl with cling film then add a layer of moss. Cut foam to fit the bowl and secure to the bowl with adhesive tape. Start by building the shape with the statice and spiraea. Wire bunches of flowers together and work towards the edge of the posy bowl. Allow some of the blooms to curl over the rim.

ℛUSTIC CHARM

❧

7 peonies
3 globe artichoke heads
1 bunch of deep pink helichrysum (strawflower or everlasting)
1 bunch of poppy seed heads
2 bunches of helipterum & 1 bunch of pink larkspur
1 bunch of oats & 1 bunch of quaking grass
3 fern leaves & 3 sprays of silver brunia
Rustic basket
Florists' dry foam & adhesive tape

The 'freshly gathered' look of this display is achieved by carefully selecting flowers and foliage to give an interesting outline and texture to the design. Secure the foam in the centre of the basket. Cut the ferns into three-inch (7cm) lengths and insert around the outside edge of the foam to create a 'collar'. Place a peony in the middle of the foam, just under the handle. Cut short bunches of smaller flowers and foliage and wire into groups. Turning the basket as you work, insert these around the edge. Build up the centre with bunches, individual flowers, artichoke and poppy heads.

$\mathcal{H}$EARTH BASKET

~

7 pink roses
12 pinky/peach helichrysum (strawflower or everlasting)
1 bunch of peach broom blooms
1 bunch of dudinea
3 sprays of peach anaphalis
Glycerined copper beech foliage
Lichen
Florists' dry foam & stub wire
Florists' adhesive tape
Log basket

$\mathcal{D}$uring the summer months, use a log basket to display a charming arrangement of pink and beige flowers. Fill the basket with several blocks of dry foam. Level off with a sharp knife and secure with tape. Divide the lichen into flat pieces and pin into the foam to cover the basket. Wire the copper beech and fix to the basket to form a central 'S' shape. Following the outline, insert single wired roses and helichrysums. Wire broom bloom, dudinea and anaphalis into bunches and use to fill in.

 59

$\mathcal{L}$AVENDER BASKET

~

1 bunch of canary grass
2 bunches of lavender
2 blocks of florists' dry foam
Reel wire
Stem tape
Cling film (plastic wrap)
Fast drying clear glue
Flat backed wall basket

$\mathcal{I}$nspired by Elizabethan garden engravings, this attractive wall design is built up by arranging alternate rows of lavender and canary grass. Fill the basket with foam and trim into a convex shape with a sharp knife. Cut down the canary grass stems to approximately one inch (2cms) and insert around the bottom edge of the basket. Next insert 4 rows of lavender and, keeping to the shape of the basket, add further rows of canary grass. For a final decorative touch, wire together a few stems of lavender and grass into a small bunch and glue to the front of the basket.

*W*ELCOME BASKET

~

20 helichrysum (strawflower or everlasting)
20 pressed hydrangea florets
2 bunches of sea lavender
Statice latifolia (Limonium latifolium)
Fragrant pot-pourri
1yd (1m) paper ribbon
Plastic bag & black reel wire
Fast drying clear glue

*T*his rustic wicker basket overflowing with colour makes a delightful display. Fill the basket with pot-pourri for a lasting fragrant arrangement. Using reel wire, bind short bundles of sea lavender to the basket handle, and also thread wired bunches of sea lavender to the rim of the basket. Cut a plastic bag to fit inside the basket and glue in place. Glue the hydrangea florets to the edge of the basket. Wait until the glue is dry and then glue the helichrysum heads into position. Loop paper ribbon around the handle and secure with a bow at both sides. Fill with your favourite pot-pourri mix.

*W*OODLAND

~

3 bunches of white larkspur
2 bunches of green love-lies-bleeding
2 bunches of broom blooms
2 bunches of willow & myrtle
2 bunches of immortelle (everlasting)
1 bunch of helichrysum (strawflower or everlasting)
9 sprays of floribunda roses
2 gnarled branches & shallow basket
Florists' foam & tape
Quick drying glue

C reate an unusual indoor garden by using a colourful selection of dried flowers. Shape foam blocks to fit tightly into the basket and secure in position with tape. Insert the larkspur and love-lies-bleeding to stand 12ins (30cms) high at the centre back. Bank one side of the basket with myrtle. Glue the two gnarled branches in position across the centre. Cut down the immortelle and broom blooms and place in position. Insert a line of helichrysum vertically through the centre and a line of roses to cut across the design.

$\mathcal{A}$UTUMN BLAZE

~

9 orange dyed protea
1 bunch of glycerined eucalyptus
2 bunches of glycerined wattle (Acacia)
1 bunch brown dyed quaking grass
Stems brown dyed grass
Reindeer moss
Florists' dry foam
Florists' reel wire & stub wire
Cling film (plastic wrap)
Basket

$\mathcal{C}$ reate this dramatic, autumnal design by combining a selection of bronze coloured foliage and grasses with bright orange proteus. Line the basket with cling film. Pack tightly with foam and secure with tape. Cut stub wires and shape into 'hairpins'. Attach the pins to the reindeer moss and insert them into the foam to cover the surface. Arrange the foliage in a random shape to complement the shape of the basket and place the proteus to make points of interest. Wire the grasses into small bunches and use to fill in.

 67

&LIZABETHAN

∾

1 bunch of pink statice
1 bunch of purple statice
1 bunch of blue larkspur
1 bunch of lime green genista
1 bunch of dark green broom
1 bunch of green dyed African daisies
5 sprays of sea holly
Florists' reel wire & wire mesh
2 vases

A brilliantly coloured collection of dried flowers makes a striking display. Place a small posy of pink statice in the smaller jug to the foreground to cleverly balance the elements of the design. Fill the base of the large vase with crunched wire mesh. Position blue larkspur at the centre back. Unbunch the broom and carefully fan out until the bunch has doubled in size. Use the broom to build up the outline. Fill in the shape with wired bunches of statice, larkspur and sea holly. Position the African daisies in the centre to complete.

$\mathcal{E}$DWARDIAN HAT

∾

5 orange dahlias
5 helichrysum (strawflower or everlasting)
Golden rod
12 ears of wheat
2 dryandra
Stems of quaking grass
Glycerined oak foliage
Moss
Florists' reel wire & stub wire
Glue & wreath wrap
Straw hat

L iven up an old straw boater with a striking floral spray. Mould the moss into an egg shape and bind carefully with wire. Cover with wreath wrap and secure to the hat with reel wire threaded through the weave. Cut stems of wheat, wire them into clumps and push into the moss. Gradually wire in dahlias, helichrysum and oak leaves to form a bunch. Group the discarded stems into bunches and wire into the base of the arrangement. To finish, glue leaves around one side of the brim.

COPPER GLOW

5 stems of pampas grass
5 stems of brown dyed oats
5 stems of glycerined eucalyptus
3 stems of Chinese lanterns
3 stems of reedmace (small bullrush)
1 dried maize/corn head (Indian corn)
Copper kettle
Florists' foam & adhesive tape
Reel wire

The warm glow of an old copper kettle complements this autumnal display of dried grasses and
flowers. Begin by wedging a block of dry foam into the kettle, allowing it to protude above the neck by 1½ins (4cms).
Secure with adhesive tape. Use the foliage to make an outline shape then soften the line by positioning the pampas
grass. Next, arrange the reedmace and Chinese lanterns
into groups and position to cover the foam at the front.
Lastly, pull back the bracts of the corn, cut the stem short
and position to follow the line of the spout.

 73

COTTAGE STYLE

5 stems of leucodendron
2 bunches of peach helichrysum (strawflower or everlasting)
2 bunches of love-in-a-mist & 2 bunches of sea lavender
2 bunches of quaking grass
1 bunch of peach dyed achillea
1 bunch of peach dyed African daisies
1 bunch of glycerined wattle (Acacia)
Woven basket
Reel & stub wire
Florists' dry foam & adhesive tape
Cling film (plastic wrap)

This delightful array of country flowers is designed to look like a freshly gathered display. Line the basket with cling film. Fill with foam and secure with tape. Cut down the stems of sea lavender and push into the foam to cover the surface. Position groups of flowers just above the height of the handle and around the perimeter of the basket. Wire flowers into mixed bunches and add to the basket. Insert brown wattle foliage to break up the solid look of the design.

 75

$\mathcal{E}$CHO

~

11 poppy seed heads
5 stems of bells of Ireland (Moluccella)
9 stems of dyed blue immortelle (everlasting)
3 oleander-leaved protea & 3 bleached palm leaves
Branches of glycerined beech leaves
Branches of glycerined oak leaves
Stems of bleached quaking grass & bleached linseed
Florists' dry foam & stub wire
1930s style vase

The bold design on this elegant vase is beautifully complemented by this dried flower arrangement. Fill the vase with dry foam. Cut down a spray of beech to twice the height of the vase and position at the back. Place the remaining foliage to make a fan shape and use poppy heads to make a central curve vertically through the display to the edge of the vase. Group the immortelle in the centre with the protea springing out from among them. Fill in with quaking grass and linseed. Wire together a few poppies, oak leaves and bells of Ireland to form a sweep over the rim of the vase.

$\mathcal{G}$OLDEN BLEND

∾

3 protea
3 open & 6 closed cones
1 maize/corn cob (Indian corn)
2 branches of hops
Ears of wheat
Strelitzia leaves (bird of paradise)
Eucalyptus & chestnut leaves
Ferns
Florists' dry foam
Plastic pinholder & fixative
Gold spray paint

$\mathcal{T}$ransform the look of a dried flower arrangement by adding a touch of gold spray paint. This display would make a welcome addition to your sitting room. Place all the items in the lid of a large cardboard box and spray with gold paint. Make sure all the surfaces are covered. Secure dry foam into the container with fixative. Position strelitzia leaves and other foliage to form an 'L' shape. Group the cones and protea in the centre and allow the hops to spill over the edge of the container.

$\mathscr{F}$ESTIVE DISPLAY

3 white candles & 8 cones
2 vine wreaths, 9½ins (24cms) and 12ins (30cms) diameter
3 artichokes & 1 bunch of poppy seed heads
5 stems of bupleurum & 3 stems of buxifolium
1 bunch of miniature everlasting & fern leaves
Rhododendron foliage & reindeer moss
Florists' 'staysoft' clay & round flat plate
Florists' stub wire, reel wire & adhesive tape
2yd (2m) of red & 1yd (1m) of tartan ribbon
Fire retardant spray & clear glue

This splendid Christmas design will last throughout the holiday. Fix clay to the centre of the plate and press in the candles. Place the large wreath over the plate and build up foliage and bupleurum at the back, leaning away from the candles. Add fern around the perimeter. Insert poppy heads, cones and moss to one side of the candles and make bows to fill the other side. Lean the small wreath against the front of the large one, and fill the centre with the remaining items. Finally, spray with fire retardant spray.

Part 3

Flowers as Food

*T*he recent emphasis on presenting food that is as good to look at as it is to eat has encouraged a revival in the art of cooking with flowers. Garnishing with flowers and herbs has long been popular and a random scattering of petals or leaves can transform the appearance of a dish, but many of the recipes in this book use flowers as a major ingredient as well. The final results are extremely good and the subtle flavours and textures that flowers can introduce to a dish suit the modern move towards light, simple flavours and fresh, natural food.

Any garden, whatever size it may be, will provide enough space to grow a selection of flowers for the kitchen. Hyssop, thyme, marjoram and rosemary can all be used for their leaves as well as their flowers. Nasturtiums and marigolds are superb in salads and add a splash of brilliant colour and a delicious spicy flavour. Roses can be used in summer puddings to add a subtle aroma as well as a pretty garnish. Elder blossoms are traditionally used to make a sparkling country drink, and scented geraniums

make the most delicious preserves, while dried flowers can be used to make fragrant teas.

The flowers you choose should be fresh, unblemished and unsprayed. Check for insects and, if you wash the flowers, do so carefully as the delicate petals can bruise easily. If you decide to experiment with different types of flowers do check first that they are edible, as some are poisonous. Remember, too, that some wild flowers are scarce, so only pick common, unprotected species.

These creative recipes add a new dimension to food preparation and certainly give the home cook the chance to experiment. Try making some of the recipes in this chapter or use flowers to liven up a favourite dish – you could be pleasantly surprised.

$\mathcal{S}$UMMER SALAD

Mixed lettuce leaves
About 36 nasturtium heads

Dressing
2 tablespoons olive oil
1 tablespoon walnut oil
1 teaspoon made French mustard
1 tablespoon white wine vinegar
Salt & ground pepper

$\mathcal{N}$asturtiums add a peppery taste to a green or mixed salad and a flash of contrasting colour. This attractive summer salad, rich in vitamin C, can be eaten as a first course or on its own.

The nasturtium flowers should be fresh, unblemished and unsprayed. Do not wash them if possible, as the petals bruise easily. Check in the long horn at the back for insects and pick off the stem. Mix the flowers with the lettuce leaves. Shake the dressing ingredients together and mix with the salad just before serving. Serves 6.

HYSSOP & BEAN SALAD

1¼lb (600g) salad potatoes, cooked and cooled
10oz (300g) french beans, cooked and cooled
2oz (60g) black olives
8oz (250g) cherry tomatoes
2 tablespoons chopped fresh hyssop flowers & leaves
Sprigs fresh hyssop flowers, to decorate

Dressing
3 tablespoons olive oil
1 tablespoon lemon juice
1 crushed garlic clove
Salt & ground pepper

In midsummer take advantage of the abundant supplies of vegetables to make this tasty and colourful salad. Gently mix all the salad ingredients together and put in an earthenware dish. Blend together the ingredients for the dressing and pour over the salad just before serving. Decorate with the brilliant-blue hyssop blooms.

GERANIUM MELON

~

1 small water melon
10 fl oz (300ml/1¼ cups) water
2½oz (75g/⅓ cup) caster sugar
2 strips lemon peel
Borage (Borago) leaves and flowers
Juice of 1 lemon & 1 lime
Scented geranium leaves and flowers

This colourful and pretty combination of fruit and flowers makes a wonderfully refreshing starter for a light lunch. Slice off the top of the water melon. Carefully extract the fruit and remove the pips. Roughly chop the fruit into cubes, and mix with the water, sugar, lemon peel and borage leaves. Transfer this mixture to a saucepan and simmer for a few minutes to allow the flavours to combine but do not let the fruit become mushy. Strain the mixture and allow to cool. Add the lemon and lime juice and spoon the mixture back into the water melon. Decorate with a few scented geranium and borage flowers and leaves and for an extra special occasion serve the melon on a bed of vine leaves. Serves 1.

ʃALAD BURNETT SAVOURY

∽

Equal amounts of cottage cheese & cream cheese
Salad burnett (burnet) leaves & flowers
Fennel flowers
Olive oil
Salt & ground pepper
Melba toast

ʃalad burnett, fennel flowers and a little black pepper combined with soft cheeses, produces this delightfully refreshing savoury which can be served as a starter or at the end of a meal. Strip the leaves from salad burnett stems and wash well. Chop the leaves finely and place in a bowl with the fennel flowers, a teaspoon of olive oil and salt and pepper to taste. Leave for 30 minutes and then add the cottage cheese and cream cheese and beat with a fork. Lightly oil the insides of ramekins or small bowls, and fill with the cheese mixture. Chill well and then turn out and decorate with fennel florets and serve with Melba toast. Serves 4.

91

ROSE VINAIGRETTE

~

1 cup rose wine vinegar
1 cup sunflower oil
1 teaspoon sugar
4 pink roses
Red & pink roses for decoration

Globe artichokes make appetising starters and look especially attractive served on a bed of rose petals with rose-petal vinaigrette. Some varieties of rose-petal are sweeter than others, so taste those you intend to use.

Cook the artichokes in boiling salted water until tender. To test, lift from the pan and pull away one of the leaves – if it comes away easily it is cooked. Drain upside down in a colander. Cut off the white bitter part at the base of each rose-petal and put in a bowl. Boil the wine vinegar in a pan and add the sugar. Pour this mixture over the rose petals and leave to stand for about 4 hours. Strain and add the sunflower oil. Pour into a glass jug and decorate with a few rose petals. Serves 4.

BORAGE SOUP

~

½lb (250g) young borage (Borago) leaves & flowers
2oz (60g/⅓ cup) short grain rice
2oz (60g/¼ cup) butter
1½ pints (900ml/3¾ cups) chicken or vegetable stock
6oz (175g/¾ cup) double cream (or fromage frais)
Seasoning to taste

This dark green soup served cold is perfect for summer dinner parties or that extra special picnic. Melt the butter in a saucepan. Add the rice and cook over a low heat for two minutes, stirring all the time. Add the stock and simmer for 15 minutes. Strip the borage leaves and flowers from the stalks and wash well. Leave aside some flowers for decoration and add the remainder to the saucepan. Simmer for a further 10 minutes. Season to taste. Allow to cool for a while, then liquidize in a blender. Pour the soup through a fine sieve into a serving tureen and allow to cool. Before serving stir in the cream or if preferred some thinned fromage frais, and decorate with the bright blue borage flowers. Serves 4.

MARIGOLD CAULIFLOWER

~

1 medium sized cauliflower
2oz (60g/¼ cup) butter
2oz (60g/½ cup) plain white flour
3oz (90g/⅓ cup)) grated cheese
½pt (300ml/1¼ cups) milk
6 heads pot marigolds
Salt & pepper

*M*arigolds are such bright and cheerful flowers, and as well as being good to look at they can also be good to eat. They have a subtle spicy flavour which can transform this favourite dish into something special. Make the white sauce in the usual manner. Carefully wash the marigold flowers in cold running water and shake dry. Reheat the white sauce and stir in the grated cheese while over the heat, but do not allow to boil. Remove from heat, and add in the marigold petals. Stir carefully. Place the lightly cooked cauliflower into a serving dish and pour the sauce over the top. Serves 4.

CHICKEN & THYME

Skinned chicken breasts
Long stems of thyme in bloom
Bunch fresh thyme
3 tablespoons corn oil
Juice of 2 lemons
Salt & pepper

*C*hicken cooked with thyme tastes delicious and this appetising dish is the perfect choice for an informal summer lunch or barbecue party. Chop or grind the bunch of thyme, and mix with the corn oil, lemon juice and seasoning in a large bowl. Add the chicken pieces to the mixture and leave to marinate for two hours, turning the chicken occasionally. Remove the chicken just before cooking and allow to drain, but make sure plenty of chopped thyme is left on the chicken pieces. Cook the chicken over a medium hot barbecue for approximately 20 minutes. For extra flavour dip the long stems of flowering thyme into the marinade and lay over the chicken while the underside is cooking.

MARIGOLD FILLETS

~

Fillets of smoked mackerel or herring
Small green lettuce

Sauce
2 tablespoons sunflower oil
4 tablespoons cider vinegar
2 heaped teaspoons grated horseradish
8 heads marigold flowers

Serve succulent smoked mackerel or herring fillets on a bed of orange marigold flowers and crisp green lettuce for a winning summer party dish. Measure the cider vinegar into a mixing bowl, add the grated horseradish and crush well with a wooden spoon. Blend in the sunflower oil and leave to infuse for 30 minutes. Wash the marigold flowers and drain well. Cut the mackerel fillets in half lengthways and arrange in a star shape on a bed of lettuce. Stir the marigold petals into the sauce and spoon some of the sauce and petals between the fillets. Serve the rest of the sauce separately. Serves 4.

$\mathcal{E}$LDERFLOWER FRITTERS

∾

Elderflower (Sambucus nigra) sprays, just open
2 eggs
2oz (60g/½ cup) plain flour
½ pt (300ml/1¼ cups) milk
Icing sugar
Oil for deep frying

$\mathcal{E}$ lderflowers, seen in abundance along the hedgerows in spring, can be used to make an interesting and unusual after dinner dessert. Examine the sprays carefully for insects, and shake well but do not wash. Sift the flour into a bowl. Make a well in the centre and drop in the egg yolks. Draw the flour into the yolks, while gradually adding the milk. Beat the batter until it is the consistency of single cream. Heat the oil in a deep pan. Dip the flower heads into the batter. Shake off the excess and, holding onto the stalk, deep fry the flower head for two minutes. Dry on kitchen paper. Cut off the stalks just before serving and dust with icing sugar. Serve hot or cold. Serves 4.

'PINK' PEARS

~

6 firm pears
½ bottle red wine
18 garden pinks (Dianthus x allwoodii)
½pt (300ml/1¼ cups) double cream
2 tablespoons milk
Sugar

This elegant dish is a perfect summer dessert. Wash the pinks carefully and shake dry. Remove the petals from 12 flowers and place in a saucepan with the wine and sugar to taste. Bring to the boil. Peel the pears, but leave on the stalks. Place in the saucepan and leave to simmer for 20 minutes, turning so that all sides colour evenly. Remove the pears, and reduce the liquid to make a thick sauce. Allow to cool. Heat the milk in a double saucepan and add the petals from the remaining 6 pinks. Heat to just below boiling point for 5 minutes. Remove from the heat and allow to stand for 15 minutes then strain the milk into a bowl. Add a teaspoon of sugar, allow to dissolve, then pour in cream and beat to a stiff consistency. Serve pears with the sauce poured over. Serves 6.

ROSE DESSERT

~

10fl oz (300ml/1¼ cups) whipping cream
(or half cream, half fromage frais)
1½ tablespoons gelatine
4 tablespoons water
2 large eggs, separated
2oz (60g/¼ cup) caster sugar
10fl oz (300ml/1¼ cups) Greek yoghurt
2 tablespoons triple-distilled rose water
Petals and flowers, to decorate

This soft light pudding is slightly scented and flavoured with roses. It combines beautifully with the tender red fruits of summer – strawberries, redcurrants, cherries and raspberries. Whip the cream lightly. Dissolve the gelatine in the water. Beat the egg yolks and sugar with an electric whisk until thick and fluffy, then beat in the yoghurt. Whisk the egg whites. Beat the cool gelatine into the egg-yolk mixture and, working rapidly, add the rose water, cream and beaten egg whites. Pour into a dish and chill for several hours before decorating. Serves 6.

ℳARIGOLD CAKE

8oz (250g/1 cup) softened butter
8oz (250g/1 cup) caster sugar
4 eggs, beaten
8oz (250g/2 cups) plain flour
1 teaspoon baking powder
Grated rind of 1 orange & 1 lemon
3 tablespoons fresh marigold petals
or 2 tablespoons dried
Granulated sugar (optional)

ℳarigold petals give a delicate flavour and a slight orange hue to this light tea-time cake. Grease and line a 2lb (1kg) loaf tin. Cream the butter with the sugar and add the beaten egg a little at a time. Sieve the flour with the baking powder and fold into the creamed mixture. Add in the orange and lemon rinds and the marigold petals. Spoon into the tin and bake in a oven preheated to 350°F (180°C or Mark 4) for about 1 hour. Sprinkle with granulated sugar about half-way through if desired. Cool for 5 minutes, then remove from the tin. Serve when just cool. This cake keeps well and can be frozen.

GERANIUM JELLY

∾

4lb (2kg) cooking apples
1¾ pints (1 litre/4 cups) water
Granulated or preserving sugar
Juice of 2 lemons
15 scented geranium leaves

There are many different types of scented geraniums but rose- and lemon-scented varieties are the best for making these delicious preserves. Serve at teatime with good bread and butter or plain scones.

Chop the apples roughly, leaving the skin, stalk and pips. Put in a large pan with the water and simmer until soft. Strain for several hours through a jelly bag or muslin; do not squeeze the fruit through or the jelly will be cloudy. Measure the juice into a preserving pan and for every pint (600ml) of juice add 1lb (450g/4 cups) of sugar. Add the lemon juice and the geranium leaves. Stir over a low heat to dissolve the sugar, then boil rapidly for about 10 minutes, until set. Quickly remove the leaves and pour into clean, warm jars.

$\mathscr{T}$RUFFLES

6oz (175g) white or plain chocolate, for centres
2 tablespoons single cream
1 egg yolk
1 tablespoon brandy &
1 tablespoon rose water
or 2 tablespoons violet liqueur
6oz (175g) white or plain chocolate, for coating
Crystallised petals to decorate

$\mathscr{T}$hese delicious truffles are made from the same basic mixture, but the rose version has a dark rose-scented truffle centre covered with white chocolate, and the violet version a white, violet-scented centre encased in plain chocolate.

Gently melt the chocolate (for the centres) into the cream. Add the egg yolk, liqueur and flavouring. Remove from the heat and cool. Roll the mixture into small balls and leave to harden. Melt the coating chocolate gently over hot water and dip each truffle in until well coated. Leave on an oiled surface and decorate with crystallised petals before set. The mixture makes about 15 truffles.

$\mathcal{E}$LDERFLOWER CUP

6 elderflower heads (Sambucus nigra)
1½lb (700g/3 cups) white sugar
3 lemons
2 tablespoons white wine vinegar
8 pints (4.5 litres) water
Elderflower sprigs, to decorate

$\mathcal{I}$n summer the frothy, creamy elderflower blossoms can be used to produce elderflower 'champagne', a sparkling, refreshing drink that can be enjoyed on any lazy summer's day. Dissolve the sugar in a little of the water heated to boiling point. Thinly pare the lemons and add the peel to the sugar. Wash the elderflower heads well to remove all insects and place in a large glass bowl. Add the sugar and peel mixture, the wine vinegar and the remaining water. Stir well, cover and leave for about 4 days in a cool place. In around 5 days it should be sparkling and ready to drink. Serve well chilled in tall glasses. Makes 9 pints (5 litres).

CLARET PUNCH

1 tablespoon caster sugar
8oz (250g) fresh strawberries
4 small strips cucumber peel
Juice of 3 lemons
3 tablespoons brandy
2 tablespoons Cointreau
2 bottles claret or similar red wine
1 bottle sparkling mineral water, soda or lemonade
Borage (Borago) flowers & mint

This delicious cherry-red wine cup is best served from a clear glass bowl to appreciate the sparkling colour and the pretty decoration. Dissolve the caster sugar in a little hot water and pour into a large bowl. Slice the strawberries if they are large, and add to the bowl together with the cucumber strips, lemon juice, brandy and Cointreau. Pour in the 2 bottles of red wine and top up with the mineral water, soda or lemonade. Chill well. When ready to serve, add ice and decorate with a liberal sprinkling of borage flowers and mint sprigs. Serves 20.

$\mathcal{T}$ISANES & TEAS

~

Good quality loose tea
Rose petals
White jasmine
Bergamot (Monarda)
Lime
Marigold
Camomile (Anthemis)

$\mathcal{A}$s well as adding scent and flavour to conventional teas, flowers can be used to make tisanes. Use 1 teaspoon of dried flowers or 3 teaspoons of fresh per cup, and steep them for about 3 or 4 minutes before drinking. Make in a jug and strain into a cup.

Make your own exotic teas by adding dried petals to loose tea. Simply mix the tea with the petals. Try strongly scented red rose petals or dried flowers from the common white jasmine. The proportion of petals to tea will depend on how strong you want the flower flavour to be. Experiment with 2 tablespoons of rose petals to 3½oz (100g/6 tablespoons) of tea, and 1 tablespoon of the stronger scented jasmine to 3½oz (100g/6 tablespoons) tea.

Part 4

Pot-Pourris

*T*he concept of perfuming a room has been with us for generations. In days gone by fresh herbs and flowers were used to mask unpleasant odours, and every large house had its own herb garden for medicinal as well as cosmetic use. Gradually the first pot-pourris were created, and many fascinating and varied recipes have been handed down over the years.

Instead of reaching for a synthetic room freshener, try making your own pot-pourri. It's fun to experiment with herbs and flowers from your own garden and you will soon build up an interesting collection of material. Leaves, grasses, nuts and seeds can be used as well as scented flowers to add interesting textures and fragrances.

Drying your chosen flowers is easy. Choose healthy blooms picked on a dry day. Spread the flowers onto sheets of newspaper and leave in a warm and airy place to dry; hang any herbs in bunches. After about a week they will feel papery and will be ready to use. Once you have all your dried ingredients ready the next step is to use a fixative in order to save the fragrance. The best fixative to use at home is powdered orris root which is widely available and very effective. Course salt and spices such as cloves, cinnamon and nutmeg also act as fixatives as well as adding an even greater variety of scents to the mixture. The final ingredient is essential oil which reinforces the natural perfume. Use this sparingly; most recipes will only need four or five drops. Mix well and leave in an airtight container for six weeks.

When making your own pot-pourri, look out for variation of colour and texture and don't be afraid to experiment with different combinations of flowers and leaves, herbs and spices to create your own special, fragrant mixtures.

GOLDEN SCENT

2 cups of dried rose petals and buds
1 cup of lemon verbena leaves
2 cups of mixed flowers including pansy, helichrysum
(strawflower or everlasting), yarrow and mimosa
½ cup of powdered orris root
1 chopped vanilla pod and 2 chopped cinnamon sticks
6 broken bay leaves
Shredded dried peel of one lemon
2 teaspoons of ground allspice
1 teaspoon of ground cloves
Oil of cloves and oil of rosemary

The flowers for this deliciously fragrant pot-pourri have been chosen for their colour and texture as well as their scent. The addition of lemon peel adds a pleasant lemony aroma.

Using a large wooden bowl, rubbed with oil of cloves, mix all the dried flowers together. Now add the other ingredients and a few drops of essential oil of rosemary. Mix well, then seal in a jar to blend and mature for six weeks, opening the jar occasionally to stir the contents.

$\mathscr{D}$AISY DAYS

∾

3 cups of pink carnation petals
3 cups of deep pink rose petals and rosebuds
2 cups of white clover flowerheads
1 cup of camomile (Anthemis) flowers
1 cup of crimson carnation petals
1 cup of broken pink and white statice flowers
1 cup of lavender seed heads
3 teaspoons of powdered orris root
½ teaspoon of powdered cloves
2 or 3 drops of lavender oil or carnation oil

$\mathscr{D}$aisy days is a delicate pot-pourri, ideal for a bedroom with its soft shades of pink and cream and subtle fresh fragrance.

Gather all your chosen flowers, putting aside a number of whole camomile and clover flowers to scatter over the finished pot-pourri. Combine all the other dried ingredients in a large bowl and mix them together gently. Carefully add 2 or 3 drops of either the oil of lavender or the oil of carnation. Store in an airtight container for six weeks, then decant.

$\int$WEET ROSE

∾

6 cups of strong scented rose petals
6 bay leaves – finely chopped
4 vanilla pods
2 tablespoons of coarse salt
(one for sprinkling over)
1 tablespoon of ground nutmeg
1 tablespoon of dried orris root powder
1 tablespoon of powdered cinnamon

This pot-pourri is made by a slightly different method, even though it uses all dried ingredients again. The addition of vanilla pods gives the pot-pourri an exotic and unusual aroma.

You will need a large, dry screw top jar for this pot-pourri. Mix all the ingredients together well, apart from the vanilla pods. Place the vanilla pods round the edge of the jar in an upright position. Now fill the jar carefully with layers of your mixture, sprinkling the salt between each layer. Finish with a final layer of salt on top. Secure the jar tightly and leave undisturbed for a month.

MEADOWSWEET

～

2 cups of pink clover flowers
2 cups of pink rose petals
2 cups of lemon mint and apple mint leaves
1 cup of marjoram and meadowsweet
1 cup of thyme and sage leaves mixed
1 cup of deep pink statice flowers
1 cup of rose geranium leaves and flowerheads
1 cup of elderflowers (Sambucus nigra)
½ cup of buchu leaves
1 tablespoon of grated lemon peel
3 teaspoons of powdered orris root
2 or 3 drops of patchouli oil

Meadowsweet is one of the prettiest recipes and looks delightful poured into low baskets with handfuls of pink clover flowers and dried grasses strewn on top. Gather all your dried flowers and herbs. Pour them into a large mixing bowl, and blend well. Now add the lemon peel, orris root and a few drops of the patchouli oil. Stir again, and store in airtight containers for about six weeks.

COTTAGE GARDEN

2 cups of mixed rose petals
1 cup of lavender flowers
1 cup of scented geranium leaves
plus a few lemon balm leaves
1 cup of mixed sweet peas, pink and purple
1 cup of pink rosebuds
1 cup of jasmine flowers
½ cup of honeysuckle flowers
½ cup of pinks 'Mrs Sinkins' (Dianthus plumarius) petals
2 teaspoons of orris root powder
2 or 3 drops of rose geranium oil
½ cup of pink helichrysum flowers

Many of the lovely flowers from your garden can be used to make this deliciously fragrant mixture. Making sure your flowers and leaves are well dried, place in a large mixing bowl and stir gently. Sprinkle on the orris root powder, which is an important preservative, and stir again. Now add your essential oil very carefully a drop at a time. Pour into airtight containers and store in a dry spot for about six weeks.

RAINBOW

∽

2 cups of red and yellow rose petals
1 cup of chopped bay and lemon balm leaves
1 cup of scented geranium leaves
2 cups of lavender flowers
1 cup of blue mallow flowers
and cornflowers
1 cup of camomile (Anthemis) flowers
½ cup of marigold flowers
½ cup of powdered cloves and allspice
1 tablespoon of dried lemon peel
2 tablespoons of powdered orris root
3 or 4 drops of lemon verbena oil

This pot-pourri makes a perfect gift. The glowing shades of the blue, red and yellow flowers and the fresh lemony aroma combine to make this a special recipe.

Collect your prepared ingredients, reserving a few whole blue mallow flowers and camomile flowers to scatter on top. Mix all the dried ingredients together in a large bowl. Add the essential oil, lemon verbena, sparingly. Mix again, then store in airtight containers for six weeks.

*L*AVENDER BLUE

∿

3 cups of lavender flowers
1 cup of rosemary mixed with
cologne mint leaves
1 cup of blue delphinium flowers
1 cup of larkspur flowers
1 cup of mauve and blue statice flowers
1 tablespoon of dried lemon peel
1 teaspoon of mixed spice
3 drops of lavender oil

*T*his mixture looks lovely in dishes with a few whole larkspur or delphinium flowers lying on top. Alternatively display in a silver bowl, to reflect the cool tones of the blue and purple hues.

After cutting bundles of fresh lavender, hang them to dry in a warm airy place, then strip the lavender flowers from the twigs. To make the pot-pourri, put all the dried ingredients into a large bowl. Mix them together well with your fingers. Add the lavender oil very carefully, one drop at a time. Mix again, then pour into airtight containers.

$\mathscr{M}$INTY GREEN

1 cup of crushed and 1 cup of small whole bay leaves
1 cup of basil and rosemary leaves
1 cup of peppermint leaves
1 cup of cologne mint leaves
1 cup of broken eucalyptus leaves
1 cup of sage and southernwood
½ cup of ground cloves
2 or 3 drops of peppermint oil

For a change gather together a selection of green leaves and mixed herbs for this fresh minty pot-pourri. You can place this mixture in bowls or use it to fill little muslin bags to hang by an open window. Mix all the dried ingredients together in a large bowl. Then very carefully add the peppermint oil, one drop at a time. Too much can ruin the delicate balance of your pot-pourri mixture, and you want to aim for a fragrance that is subtle but not overpowering. Stir the ingredients well making sure the oil is absorbed. Pour into airtight containers and store in a warm dry place for six weeks. When displaying, add a few pressed leaves for interest and texture.

SWEET HONEYSUCKLE

~

3 cups of dried marigold flowers
2 cups of honeysuckle
2 cups of gold and yellow rose petals
1 cup of mimosa flowers
1 cup of orange and gold carnation petals
1 cup of golden rod flowers
1 cup of yellow statice flowers
1 tablespoon of dried orange peel
2 teaspoons of powdered orris root
1 teaspoon of mixed spice
2 or 3 drops of sandalwood oil

*M*arigold, honeysuckle, mimosa and other lovely flowers combine to make this warm gold and amber pot-pourri. Reserve a few golden rod or yellow statice flowers before you start to scatter on the prepared mixture later. Mix together all the dried ingredients, then add a couple of drops of sandalwood essential oil very carefully. Store in airtight boxes for six weeks.

RED ROYAL

3 cups of crimson rose petals
3 cups of clove carnation petals
1 cup of deep purple pansies
1 cup of rosemary leaves and
lavender flowers
1 tablespoon of ground cloves
1 tablespoon of powdered cinnamon
1 tablespoon of powdered orris root
1 tablespoon of powdered mint leaves
1 tablespoon of powdered bay leaves
3 or 4 drops of rose oil
A few whole rosebuds to scatter over

Rich crimson and purple flowers add depth and excitement to this exotic recipe. Old fashioned rose varieties are particularly suitable as they hold their perfume and colour so well. Place your chosen flowers and herbs into a large bowl and mix gently. If you decide to use the rose oil, add a couple of drops at a time and stir in well. Place in an airtight container for about six weeks, giving the odd shake. Decant into china dishes.

ORIGINAL LAVENDER

4 cups of lavender flowers
2 cups of dried thyme
2 cups of lemon mint leaves
½ cup of coarse salt
1 tablespoon of powdered cloves
1 tablespoon of caraway seeds
1 tablespoon of dried lemon peel
3 or 4 drops of lavender oil
Small quantity of blue borage (Borago) flowers

Lavender must be one of the best known and loved of all scents. This simple pot-pourri mixture can be used to fill sachets and linen bags to keep clothes and linen fresh and sweet. Gather your ingredients together and, if some of the leaves appear too large, tear them in half. Place them in a large bowl and mix gently, making sure the salt is combined. Carefully add a few drops of essential lavender oil. Stir again, then pour into airtight containers and store for about six weeks giving the odd shake.

$\int$PRING MEMORY

~

2 cups of red and golden wallflowers
2 cups of mixed daffodils and jonquils
1 cup of mimosa flowers
1 cup of mixed freesia flowers
1 cup of azalea flowers
2 cups of mixed tulip petals
1 cup of lemon thyme
1 cup of variegated pineapple mint
1 teaspoon of dried lemon peel
3 teaspoons of powdered orris root
3 or 4 drops of citronella oil

This lovely pot-pourri incorporates many spring flowers. Its pretty shades and interesting textures will light up a dull corner of your home. Sort through your prepared ingredients, putting by a few whole mimosa and wallflower heads for later. Combine the remainder of the dried flowers, mint, orris root and thyme, mixing them gently in a large bowl. Next add the citronella oil, a few drops at a time. Put the mixture into airtight containers and place in a warm and dry position for six weeks.

$\mathcal{F}$OREST WALK

~

3 cups of well dried pine shavings
3 cups of small pine cones
2 cups of mixed nuts
1 cup of acorns, very well dried
1 cup of shredded bay leaves
1 cup of cinnamon bark
2 teaspoons of dried orange peel
1 teaspoon of mixed spice
3 teaspoons of orris root powder
1 cup of golden rod or yellow statice
2 or 3 drops of pine oil

$\mathcal{T}$his mixture will fill your room with an invigorating fresh pine fragrance. Bowls of this pot-pourri look very effective displayed against a polished wood surface, with a handful of acorns and golden rod or yellow statice on top. Check through your prepared ingredients, discarding any nuts or cones that may show a trace of damp. Mix all the dried items together in a large bowl. Next add two or three drops of the essential pine oil. Mix well, then transfer to dry airtight containers for six weeks.

147

HARVEST TIME

~

3 cups of crimson rose petals
3 cups of gold and orange rose petals
2 cups of golden rod flowers
1 cup of lemon balm leaves and basil
1 cup of seed heads, wheat or corn
1 cup of peppermint leaves
2 tablespoons of coriander seeds
1 teaspoon of powdered cinnamon
3 teaspoons of orris root powder
2 or 3 drops of sandalwood oil

Harvest shades of crimson, amber and gold combine to make this unusual and attractive pot-pourri. The addition of sandalwood oil leaves a warm lingering woody fragrance.

Place all the dried flowers and seed heads into a large bowl. If using wheat or corn, take off some of the ears, making sure they are perfectly dry. Combine the ingredients ensuring the orris root powder is thoroughly mixed in. Add two or three drops of the essential oil and mix well. Pour into airtight containers for six weeks, then decant.

$\mathcal{A}$UTUMN BREEZE

∾

1 cup of bayberry bark
1 cup of buchu leaves
1 cup of small bay leaves
1 cup of eucalyptus leaves
1 cup of pine wood shavings
1 cup of dried seed heads
5 or 6 strips of eucalyptus bark
1 cup of small pine cones
2 tablespoons of coarse salt
1 tablespoon of dried lemon peel
1 tablespoon of mixed spice
6 whole cloves
2 or 3 drops of lemon grass oil

$\mathcal{T}$his masculine recipe has a clean lemon and pine aroma and looks very attractive poured into a simple polished box with a handful of gold helichrysum and cones sprinkled on top. Before you start make sure all the ingredients are completely dry. Mix all the ingredients together in a large bowl. Add the oil sparingly, mix again, and store for six weeks.

$\mathcal{L}$AVENDER BOTTLES

∾

15-20 long stems of fresh lavender
Ribbon or strong string

$\mathcal{L}$ avender bottles are easy to make and are a pretty and unusual way of keeping clothes fresh and sweet smelling. The method is quite simple but you may need a little practice. Gather together a bunch of long stemmed fresh lavender and tie a thin piece of string or ribbon directly under the lavender heads. Gently bend each stem back separately to encase the lavender heads and make a small cage. Tie another length of ribbon around the stems. Leave a loop of ribbon hanging and allow the lavender to dry naturally before using.

To make a simple and inexpensive gift, arrange the lavender bottles in a pretty basket and tie with matching ribbon. Try weaving a length of ribbon through the lavender stems to make the bottle more secure. Pull the ribbon tighter at the top and bottom of the bottle but looser around the centre to ensure an even shape.

$\int$CENTED BAGS

1 cup of strongly scented rose petals
1 cup of lavender
½ cup of lemon verbena leaves
½ cup of crushed rosemary
¼ cup of powdered orris root
2 crushed cinnamon sticks
Few drops of essential rose oil

his simple but deliciously fragrant mixture is perfect for making into sachets and scented bags to place between laundry and bedding. The simplest bag can be made by filling a lace handkerchief with a scoop of potpourri and tying with a piece of ribbon. Pretty bags can also be made from scraps of material you already have. Take a strip of fabric about 19ins (48cms) long by 4ins (10cms) wide. With right sides facing fold the strip in half and sew a narrow seam up both sides. Turn the right way out, fill with pot-pourri, and tie around the neck with ribbon. To make the pot-pourri, mix all the dry ingredients together in a large bowl. Add a few drops of oil until the scent is right. Store in an airtight box for 2 weeks.

$\mathcal{P}$RETTY PARCELS

∾

Coloured tissue paper
Gift tags
Dried or fresh flowers to decorate
Pot-pourri mixture (Sweet Rose page 126)
String or ribbon

$\mathcal{A}$ very inexpensive but effective way of gift-wrapping pot-pourri is to place one or more scoopfuls of your favourite mixture onto a piece of triple-thickness coloured tissue paper. Carefully bring the edges up to the middle and tie them with string or pretty coloured ribbon, to make a little bag. Pastel shades of tissue paper look very pretty, especially if you add a matching label or gift tag. For a special effect attach a small cluster of dried flowers, or even a fresh flower to the ribbon or string securing the bag. A small group of multi-coloured parcels placed in a basket or similar container would look delightful for an unusual gift. If you keep a stock of ribbon, gift tags and tissue paper you can create a simple but attractive gift whenever the need arises.

$\mathcal{I}NDEX$